Planning for Learning through Autumn

by Rachel Sparks Linfield and Penny Coltman. Illustrated by Cathy Hughes

Contents

Published by Practical Pre-School Books, A Division of MA Education Ltd,
St Jude's Church, Dulwich Road, Herne Hill, London, SE24 0PB Tel: 020 7738 5454

www.practicalpreschoolbooks.com

Revised (3rd edition) © MA Education Ltd 2013. Reprinted 2012.
Revised edition © MA Education Ltd 2008. First edition © Step Forward Publishing Limited 2001.

Front cover image taken by Lucie Carlier © MA Education Ltd.
Back cover images (left-right) © iStockphoto.com/Dale Hogan, Lucie Carlier © MA Education Ltd.

Planning for L   280-37-3

Making plans

Child-friendly Planning

The purpose of planning is to make sure that all children enjoy a broad and balanced experience of learning. Planning should be flexible, useful and child-friendly. It should reflect opportunities available both indoors and outside. Plans form part of a planning cycle in which practitioners make observations, assess and plan.

Children benefit from reflective planning that takes into account the children's current interests and abilities and also allows them to take the next steps in their learning. Plans should make provision for activity that promotes learning and a desire to imagine, observe, communicate, experiment, investigate and create.

Plans should include a variety of types of activity. Some will be adult-initiated or adult-led, that focus on key skills or concepts. These should be balanced with opportunities for child-initiated activity where the children take a key role in the planning. In addition there is a need to plan for the on-going continuous provision areas such as construction, sand and water, malleable materials, small world, listening area, role-play and mark-making. Thought also needs to be given to the enhanced provision whereby an extra resource or change may enable further exploration, development and learning.

The outdoor environment provides valuable opportunities for children's learning. It is vital that plans value the use of outdoor space.

The UK Frameworks

Within the UK a number of frameworks exist to outline the provision that children should be entitled to receive. Whilst a variety of terms and labels are used to describe the Areas of Learning there are key principles which are common to each document. For example they advocate that practitioners' planning should be personal based on observations and knowledge of the specific children within a setting. They acknowledge that young children learn best when there is scope for child-initiated activity. In addition it is accepted that young children's learning is holistic. Although within the documents Areas of Learning are presented separately to ensure that key areas are not over-looked, within settings, children's learning will combine areas. Thus the Areas of Learning are perhaps of most use for planning, assessment and recording.

Focused area plans

The plans you make for each day will outline areas of continuous provision and focused, adult-led activities. Plans for focused-area activities need to include aspects such as:

● resources needed;
● the way in which you might introduce activities;
● individual needs;
● the organisation of adult help;
● size of the group;
● timing;
● safety;
● key vocabulary.

Identify the learning and the Early Learning Goals that each activity is intended to promote. Make a note of any assessments or observations that you are likely to carry out. After carrying out the activities, make notes on your plans to say what was particularly successful, or any changes you would make another time.

A final note

Planning should be seen as flexible. Not all groups meet every day, and not all children attend every day. Any part of the plan can be used independently, stretched over a longer period or condensed to meet the needs of any group. You will almost certainly adapt the activities as children respond to them in different ways and bring their own ideas, interests and enthusiasms. The important thing is to ensure that the children are provided with a varied and enjoyable curriculum that meets their individual developing needs.

Making plans

Using the book

Read the section which outlines links to the Early Learning Goals (pages 4-6) and explains the rationale for focusing on 'Autumn'.

The chart on page 7 gives an example format for weekly planning. It provides opportunity to plan for the on-going continuous provision, as well as more focused activities.

Use pages 8 to 19 to select from a wide range of themed, focused activities that recognise the importance of involving children in practical activities and giving them opportunities to follow their own interests. For each 'Autumn' theme, two activities are described in detail as examples to help you in your planning and preparation. Key vocabulary, questions and learning opportunities are identified. Use the activities as a basis to:

- extend current and emerging interests and capabilities
- engage in sustained conversations
- stimulate new interests and skills

Find out on page 20 how the Autumn activities can be brought together within an Autumn Gallery.

Use page 21 for ideas of resources to collect or prepare. Remember that the books listed are only suggestions. It is likely that you will already have within your setting a variety of other books that will be equally useful.

The activity overview chart on page 23 can be used either at the planning stage or after each theme has been completed. It will help you to see at a glance which aspects of children's development are being addressed and alert you to the areas which may need greater input in the future.

As children take part in the activities, their learning will progress. 'Collecting evidence' on page 22 explains how you might monitor each child's achievements.

There is additional material to support the working partnership of families and children in the form of a reproducible Family page found inside the back cover.

It is important to appreciate that the ideas presented in this book will only be a part of your planning. Many activities that will be taking place as routine in your group may not be mentioned. For example, it is assumed that sand, dough, water, puzzles, role-play, floor toys, technology and large scale apparatus are part of the ongoing early years experience. Role-play areas, stories, rhymes, singing, and group discussion times are similarly assumed to be happening in each week although they may not be a focus for described activities.

Using the 'Early Learning Goals'

The principles that are common to each of the United Kingdom curriculum frameworks for the early years are described on page 2. It is vital that, when planning for children within a setting, practitioners are familiar with the relevant framework's content and organisation for areas of learning. Regardless however, of whether a child attends a setting in England, Northern Ireland, Scotland or Wales they have a right to provision for all areas of learning. The children should experience activities which encourage them to develop their communication and language; personal, social, emotional, physical, mathematical and creative skills. They should have opportunities within literacy and be encouraged to understand and explore their world.

Within the Statutory Framework for the Early Years Foundation Stage (2012), Communication and Language; Physical Development and Personal, Social and Emotional Development are described as Prime Areas of Learning that are 'particularly crucial for igniting children's curiosity and enthusiasm for learning, and for building their capacity to learn, form relationships and thrive' (page 4, DfE 2012). The Specific Areas of Learning are Literacy, Mathematics, Understanding the World and Expressive Arts and Design.

For each Area of Learning the Early Learning Goals (ELGs) describe what children are expected to be able to do by the time they enter Year 1. These goals, detailed on pages 4 to 7, have been used throughout this book to show how activities relating to 'Autumn' could link to these expectations. For example, for Personal, Social and Emotional Development one aim relates to the development of children's 'self-confidence and self-awareness'. Activities suggested which provide the opportunity for children to do this have the reference PSE1. This will enable you to see which parts of the Early Learning Goals are covered for a given theme and to plan for areas to be revisited and developed.

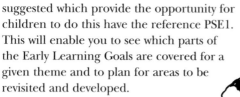

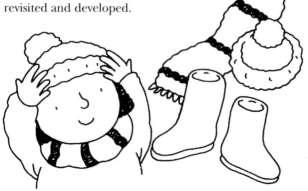

In addition, an activity may be carried out to develop a range of different Early Learning Goals. For example, when using climbing equipment, to be squirrels climbing trees, the children will develop control and co-ordination which is part of PD1. In addition, they will use their imaginations, aiding the development of Expressive Arts and Design. Thus, whilst adult-focused activities may have clearly defined goals at the planning stage, it must be remembered that as children take on ideas and initiate their own learning and activities, goals may change.

The Prime Areas of Learning
Communication and Language

Listening and attention: children listen attentively in a range of situations. They listen to stories, accurately anticipating key events and respond to what they hear with relevant comments, questions or actions. They give their attention to what others say and respond appropriately, while engaged in another activity. (CL1)

Understanding: children follow instructions involving several ideas or actions. They answer 'how' and 'why' questions about their experiences and in response to stories or events. (CL2)

Speaking: children express themselves effectively, showing awareness of listeners' needs. They use past, present and future forms accurately when talking about events that have happened or are to happen in the future. They develop their own narratives and explanations by connecting ideas or events. (CL3)

'Autumn' provides many opportunities for children to enjoy listening, understanding and speaking. When the children go on a walk to detect signs of Autumn; discuss how it feels to be outside in an Autumn wind or help to make plans for the Autumn Gallery they will talk about events in the past, the present and the future. When discussing harvest and Autumn leaves, or when listening to stories about Bonfire Night and the wind, children will have the opportunity to listen and to ask questions. Identifying fruits in a display from spoken clues, or being the wind as they blow paper around obstacles according to spoken directions, will allow the children to follow instructions.

Physical Development

Moving and handling: children show good control and co-ordination in large and small movements. They move confidently in a range of ways, safely negotiating space. They handle equipment and tools effectively, including pencils for writing. (PD1)

Health and self-care: children know the importance for good health of physical exercise, and a healthy diet, and talk about ways to keep healthy and safe. They manage their own basic hygiene and personal needs successfully, including dressing and going to the toilet independently. (PD2)

'Autumn' offers many opportunities for children to enjoy movement activities and to handle tools and equipment. When children move like fireworks, a kite in the wind or animals going into hibernation, they can develop and demonstrate control and co-ordination. Printing with leaves, helping to prepare fruit for a snack and blow painting will allow children to use small equipment and promote the development of fine motor skills. In addition, any of the described literacy activities where children write will also contribute to the development of 'handling' skills. Areas such as basic hygiene and going to the toilet independently, however, will be part of on-going, daily activity and, as a result, PD2 is not used within the described Autumn activities for Physical Development.

Personal, Social and Emotional Development

Self-confidence and self-awareness: children are confident to try new activities, and say why they like some activities more than others. They are confident to speak in a familiar group, will talk about their ideas, and will choose the resources they need for their chosen activities. They say when they do or don't need help. (PSE1)

Managing feelings and behaviour: children talk about how they and others show feelings, talk about their own and others' behaviour, and its consequences, and know that some behaviour is unacceptable. They work as part of a group or class, and understand and follow the rules. They adjust their behaviour to different situations, and take changes of routine in their stride. (PSE2)

Making relationships: children play co-operatively, taking turns with others. They take account of one another's ideas about how to organise their activity. They show sensitivity to others' needs and feelings, and form positive relationships with adults and other children. (PSE3)

'Autumn' offers many opportunities, both for child-initiated and adult-led activities, that will develop children personally, socially and emotionally. When considering how to behave on the Autumn walk, and when making rules for visitors in the Autumn Gallery, children have the opportunity to consider what is acceptable behaviour. Collaborating to make an Autumn display, to play in the role-play grocer's shop and to act out Aesop's tale of the 'Wind and the Sun' will encourage children to make relationships. Many of the areas described within the ELGs for Personal, Social and

Emotional Development though, will be covered on an almost incidental basis. Any activity that involves making choices, or showing initiative, will promote self-confidence and self-awareness.

The Specific Areas of Learning
Literacy

Reading: children read and understand simple sentences. They use phonic knowledge to decode regular words and read them aloud accurately. They also read some common irregular words. They demonstrate understanding when talking with others about what they have read. (L1)

Writing: children use their phonic knowledge to write words in ways which match their spoken sounds. They also write some irregular common words. They write simple sentences which can be read by themselves and others. Some words are spelt correctly and others are phonetically plausible. (L2)

Activities for Autumn based on picture books and stories will provide opportunities for the children to read using both their phonic knowledge and memories of common, irregular words. Discussions of the stories will help children to understand and to develop their vocabularies. Activities, such as writing descriptive words on Autumn leaf shaped paper; contributing a line to a group Autumn poem; writing words for an Autumn fruit acrostic; or making a poster to advertise the Autumn gallery will encourage children to explore the sounds within words and to enjoy the early stages of writing.

Mathematics

Numbers: children count reliably with numbers from 1 to 20, place them in order and say which number is one more or one less than a given number. Using quantities and objects, they add and subtract two single-digit numbers and count on or back to find the answer. They solve problems, including doubling, halving and sharing. (M1)

Shape, space and measures: children use everyday language to talk about size, weight, capacity, position, distance, time and money to compare quantities and objects and to solve problems. They recognise, create and describe patterns. They explore characteristics of everyday objects and shapes and use mathematical language to describe them. (M2)

Activities for Autumn provide many opportunities for children to count, to measure and to explore shape and space. Playing a conker collecting game, using number rhymes and buying and selling harvest foods encourages children to count and to compare. Investigations of Autumn leaves stimulate counting and grouping. The use of conkers, as weights, allows children to use non-standard measures and gain awareness of mass. Role-play areas such as the grocer's shop highlight the use of numbers in everyday life.

Understanding the World

People and communities: children talk about past and present events in their own lives and in the lives of family members. They know that other children don't always enjoy the same things, and are sensitive to this. They know about similarities and differences between themselves and others, and among families, communities and traditions. (UW1)

The world: children know about similarities and differences in relation to places, objects, materials and living things. They talk about the features of their own immediate environment and how environments might vary from one another. They make observations of animals and plants and explain why some things occur, and talk about changes. (UW2)

Technology: children recognise that a range of technology is used in places such as homes and schools. They select and use technology for particular purposes. (UW3)

To understand their world children need times to gain knowledge, to explore and to relate what they discover to both previously held ideas and future learning. Clearly activities relating to 'Autumn' offer valuable opportunities to discover facts about Autumn leaves and fruits, hibernating animals and wind effects. When exploring breads for harvest, and Autumn leaves and fruits, children will be able to make comparisons and notice similarities and differences. When researching animals that hibernate, or taking photos of trees with changing leaves, children have the opportunity to use technology. Technology will also feature in role-play as well as being part of the on-going, daily provision. Discussions with parents about harvest celebrations, which they experienced as children, will provide opportunity to consider events from the past.

Expressive Arts and Design

Exploring and using media and materials: children sing songs, make music and dance, and experiment with ways of changing them. They safely use and explore a variety of materials, tools and techniques, experimenting with colour, design, texture, form and function. (EAD1)

Being imaginative: children use what they have learnt about media and materials in original ways, thinking about uses and purposes. They represent their own ideas, thoughts and feelings through design and technology, art, music, dance, role-play and stories. (EAD2)

Whilst involved in activities for Autumn, children will experience working with a variety of materials, tools and techniques as they paint Autumn scenes, make collages of fireworks and print with fruits. When doing actions and using percussion during the singing of 'Autumn leaves are falling down'; using shakers to make wind sounds or enjoying play in the role-play tree house children have the chance to be imaginative. Throughout all the activities children should be encouraged to talk about what they see and feel as they communicate their ideas in painting, collage, music and role-play.

Note

The Early Learning Goals raise awareness of key aspects within any child's development for each Area of Learning. It is important to remember that these goals are reached through a combination of adult and child-initiated activity within Early Years settings and also a child's home life. Thus, it is vital that goals are shared by practitioners and parents, and children are given every opportunity to develop throughout their Early Years Foundation Stage at home and within a setting.

Example chart to aid planning in the EYFS

Week beginning:	Monday	Tuesday	Wednesday	Thursday	Friday
FOCUSED ACTIVITIES					
Focus Activity 1:					
Focus Activity 2:					
Stories and rhymes					
CONTINUOUS PROVISION (Indoor)					
Collage					
Construction (large)					
Construction (small)					
ICT					
Imaginative play					
Listening					
Malleable materials					
Mark making					
Painting					
Role play					
Sand (damp)					
Sand (dry)					
Water					
CONTINUOUS PROVISION (Outdoor)					
Construction					
Creative play					
Exploratory play					
Gross motor					
ENHANCED PROVISION (Indoor)					
ENHANCED PROVISION (Outdoor)					

Theme 1: Detecting Autumn

Communication and Language
- Go on an Autumn walk to detect signs of Autumn. Talk about the changes children see. Encourage the use of descriptive vocabulary to describe observations. (CL3)
- Show children pictures of a scene in Summer and Autumn. Ask children to compare trees, weather, people's clothes and so on. How many changes can the children spot? (CL3)

Physical Development
- Encourage children to make shapes with their bodies like animals going into hibernation. Ask them to scamper like squirrels and as you count to 10 they should slowly curl into a tiny ball ready to sleep for the winter. (PD1)
- Outside encourage children to be animals searching for places where they can hibernate. (PD1)

Personal, Social and Emotional Development
- Encourage children to care for their environment. Discuss the need to be 'gentle giants' and not tread on minibeasts, to take care of plants and to leave places we visit as we would wish to find them. When on an Autumn walk, look out for areas where we need to take care. If appropriate, talk about the country code. (PSE2)
- Work collaboratively to make an Autumn display of items collected on the Autumn walk and paintings of signs of Autumn. Explain that the display will be useful for the Autumn Gallery that they will make during the final week of Autumn themed activities. (PSE3)

Literacy
- Read an Autumn poem such as 'Misty' in *Out and About* by Shirley Hughes. Use this as the stimulus to write a group poem beginning with the words 'Autumn is.....'. Encourage each child to write their own idea on an A3 piece of paper. Combine the pages to make a big book poem. (L2)
- Enjoy sharing stories that feature Autumn. (L1)

Mathematics
- Make a pelmanism-type game in which children can match the numbers of autumn leaves, squirrels, acorns and conkers. Use numbers up to five. Encourage children to count aloud the objects on the cards. (M1)
- Adapt counting songs and rhymes for Autumn (see activity opposite). (M1)

- Cut out 30 conkers from brown card. With a small group take it in turns to roll a dice and collect conkers. The 'squirrel' who collects the most conkers is the winner. (M1)

Understanding the World
- Use books and the internet to research animals that hibernate, such as hedgehogs. (UW2, 3)
- In preparation for the Harvest theme, bake some harvest bread (see activity opposite). Encourage children to describe what they see, smell and, where appropriate, taste. (NB Children with coeliac disease may not eat bread which contains gluten.) (UW2)
- Use a digital camera to start to record Autumn changes. (UW3)

Expressive Arts and Design
- Use powder paints to make paintings of Autumn. Encourage children to mix Autumn colours. (EAD1)
- Start a collaborative display of a tree in Autumn. Leaves can be made by drawing around children's hands on Autumn coloured paper and cutting them out. (EAD1)

Activity: An Autumn finger rhyme

Learning opportunity: Developing a familiarity with numbers one to five.

Early Learning Goal: Mathematics. Numbers.

Resources: None.

Organisation: Whole group.

What to do: Use a 'carpet time' to learn and enjoy this rhyme. After each verse count the fingers which the children are holding up to reinforce number awareness.

5 red squirrels bushy and sweet,
(Hold up fingers of one hand)
Are looking for some nuts to keep,
(Hand in front of eyes – looking all around)
One red squirrel climbs a tree
(Mime climbing)
Shuts his eyes and falls asleep,
(Pretend to be asleep)
So that leaves four red squirrels
(Clap, clap, clap, clap, then hold up 4 fingers ready for next verse)

Activity: Baking bread

Learning opportunity: Describing experiences using a variety of senses.

Early Learning Goal: Understanding the World. The world.

Resources: See recipe.

Organisation: Small group.

Key vocabulary: Bread, flour, water, yeast, sugar, salt, dough, knead, rise, bake.

What to do: For a dozen rolls:
3 teaspoons of dried yeast
600ml (1 pint) warm milk
900g (2lb) strong flour
2 teaspoons salt

Sprinkle the yeast on the milk and leave in a warm place for 15 minutes until frothy.

Put the flour and salt in a bowl.

Make a well in the centre and pour in the yeast and milk mixture.

Mix well to make a dough.

Turn onto a lightly floured surface and encourage the children to knead it well for several minutes. Put the dough in a clean bowl.

Cover with a clean tea towel and leave the dough in a warm place for about an hour until it has doubled in size.

Divide the dough into pieces for the children to use. They could make it into animal shapes, such as hedgehogs or crocodiles.

Leave the finished 'rolls' in a warm place for about half an hour before baking.

Bake at 230ºC mark 8 for ten minutes, then 200ºC, mark 6 for ten minutes. Cool on a rack.

As the children make the bread ask a variety of open-ended questions, encouraging children to use as many senses as possible. What does the flour feel like? Does the smell of yeast remind you of anything? What differences can you see after the dough has been left to rise? What can you smell as the bread bakes? What do you think of its taste?

Display

Cover a table with an Autumn coloured cloth. Display an Autumn picture in the centre. Over the weeks add objects collected by the children which indicate the coming of Autumn. Display the collaborative 'Tree of Hands' in an area to which other trees can be added as seasons change. Put up the Autumn paintings as a giant patchwork and display the group's 'big book poem' near by.

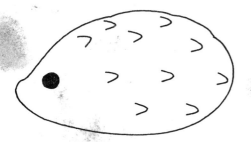

Theme 2: Harvest

Communication and Language

- Talk about harvest as a time to say thank you for foods we eat. As a group make a list of foods for which to say thank you. (CL1)
- Look at pictures of foods eaten or grown in different countries. Discuss similarities and differences. Have children eaten the foods? What do they taste like? (CL3)
- Read the *Enormous Turnip* (any version, eg Ladybird) As a group retell the story. (CL1)

Physical Development

- Talk about harvesting and the types of machines farmers use to harvest. Ask children to mime being harvesting machines. Help them to discuss what they are harvesting and how the machine works. Encourage big movements at varying speeds and levels. (PD1)
- Play the shopping game (see activity opposite). (PD1)

Personal, Social and Emotional Development

- When artefacts made by children are added to the ongoing Autumn display, encourage children to treat them carefully. Talk about the need to respect the property of others. (PSE2)
- Set up the role play area as a grocer's shop or market stall using pretend foods. Encourage children to make labels for the different foods using pictures or writing. Use the shop to take on the roles of customers and shop keepers. (PSE3)

Literacy

- Together make a collection of words to describe foods. Write each word on a separate card. Invite children to select a card, read the word and name a food that fits the description. Over the weeks encourage children to add more words to the collection. (L1)
- Encourage children to make their first name's initial letter from salt dough (see recipe opposite). (L2)
- Encourage children to make price tags for the foods in the role play shop, for example, apple – 4 pence. (L2)

Mathematics

- When using salt dough introduce and reinforce comparative vocabulary – shorter, shortest, longer, longest. (M2)
- Through buying and selling in the role play area encourage children to use numbers up to 10 and to solve simple problems showing awareness of addition. (M1)
- Look at bread products of different shapes, for example, a baguette, a tin loaf, some pitta bread or a roll. Talk about the different shapes of the breads. Cut a slice of each. What shapes are the slices? (M2)

Understanding the World

- Closely observe a range of common vegetables and fruits. Sort according to shape and colour. (UW2)
- Use salt dough to make models of common fruits and vegetables (see activity opposite). (UW2)
- Invite parents to talk to the group about harvest celebrations they experienced when they were children. (UW1)

Expressive Arts and Design

- Encourage children to make baskets from paper bun cases. Add a paper strip handle. Fill the baskets with harvest gifts made from scrap materials or dough or by cutting out pictures of foods from magazines. (EAD2)
- Make up a dance showing the change from seed to harvest. (EAD2)

Activity: Salt dough models

Learning opportunity: Investigating the properties of dough and developing language to describe observations.

Early Learning Goal: Understanding the World. The world.

Resources: Session 1: prepared dough, table covered with plastic cloth tall enough for children to stand to work.

Session 2: paints in fruit colours.

Organisation: Up to 8 children.

Key vocabulary: Squash, stretch, squeeze, sticky, soft, hard.

What to do: Prepare some dough according to the following recipe:

2 cups plain flour
1 cup salt
1 tablespoon cooking oil
1/4 cup lukewarm water

Mix together the flour and salt. Add the oil and water and knead thoroughly. (NB Children with broken skin, such as open cuts or eczema, on their hands should not work with salt dough without protection from disposable surgical gloves.)

Use a floor covering so that children may be involved in the preparation of the dough without worrying about too much mess. Talk about the textures of the flour and salt and the changes which happen as the liquid water and oil are added.

Provide each child with a ball of dough. Ask them to describe what it feels like. How can they change its shape? Can they roll the ball into a long sausage?

Show a range of common fruits. Discuss what they look like.

Ask children to use their dough to make a model of one of the pieces of fruit.

After the models have been baked, talk about the changes which have happened. How has the dough changed?

Encourage children to paint their fruit being careful to match colours.

Activity: The shopping game

Learning opportunity: Working together collaboratively, listening to instructions.

Early Learning Goal: Physical Development. Moving and handling.

Organisation: Whole group either outside or in a hall where the children can run. Children should sit in a large circle.

Key vocabulary: Apple, plum, pear, carrot, potato, bread, words to indicate ways to move.

What to do: Allocate the name of an item of food from the key vocabulary list to each child in the circle (up to 4 children could be each item).

Tell a story about Mrs Brown going shopping for food to fill a harvest basket. Include a mention of the different foods in a variety of ways, for example 'along the way Mrs Brown was tempted by the juicy red apples and she could not resist eating one of them; Just as she was about to go home she realised she had not got enough plums to make the jam...' As children hear their food word they stand up and move round the circle in a clockwise direction and sit down when they get back to their place. Additional instructions can be given in story form to indicate to the children how they should move, for example, the potatoes made Mrs Brown's bag so heavy that she was struggling to walk; the bread shop was about to close so she hurried along.

Display

Display the salt dough fruits in a large basket and add to the Autumn table.

Make a thank you display. Make a large 'Thank you' label to display on a table and invite children to think about the types of food for which they want to say thank you. Ask them to make models of this food with playdough, draw pictures or bring in food wrappers or labels to add to the display during the week.

Theme 3: Autumn Leaves

Communication and Language

- Talk about the way some trees' leaves change over Autumn. Talk about the changes in colour and texture. (CL1)
- Make up a group story about a teddy lost in a wood in Autumn. Encourage children to think about the rustle of leaves and the way Teddy uses the leaves to keep warm at night. (CL3)

Physical Development

- Press leaves firmly into self-hardening clay which has been pre-cut into round or oval shapes. Allow to dry and display next to the original leaves. (PD1)
- Enjoy using leaves to make prints with paint (see activity opposite). (PD1)

Personal, Social and Emotional Development

- Provide opportunities for children to share and take turns when printing with leaves. (PSE3)
- Use scissors with a zig-zag cutting edge to cut out a variety of shapes and colours of Autumn leaves. Cut each leaf into two. Give pairs of children a handful of leaf pieces. Encourage them to work together to match the pieces. (PSE3)

Literacy

- Look at a collection of Autumn leaves. Ask children to suggest words which describe their shape, colour, texture and sound. Write the words on a large leaf-shaped piece of paper. (L1)
- Make a collection of things which begin with the sound 'l'. Provide each child with an 'l' shaped piece of paper. Ask them to fill the letter with words and drawings or pictures from mail order catalogues of objects which begin with that sound. (L1)

Mathematics

- Sort Autumn leaves according to their shape, colour, size and edges. (M2)
- Make repeating leaf patterns. (M2)
- Repeat the conker game from the Detecting Autumn theme but with paper leaves. As a variation make a dice with any six numbers from 1 to 10. (M1)

Understanding the World

- Show children pictures of trees common to your local area. Discuss what the leaves on two of the trees look like. Go outside and try to find leaves for

the two trees. Inside, use coloured chalks to make close observational drawings of the leaves. In a well ventilated area, away from children, spray the finished pictures with fixative or hair spray to prevent smudging. (UW2)

- Prepare a collection of 'half leaf' templates, and some folded pieces of A4 paper in a range of autumn colours. Show the children how to lay the template along the paper fold. Draw around it and cut along this line to make a complete leaf. Add them to the collaborative display. Compare the leaves with real ones. (UW2)
- Take a digital photo of a deciduous tree. Over the weeks take photos to show the way Autumn leaves change colour and fall from the branches. (UW3)

Expressive Arts and Design

- Use Autumn leaves to make pictures of animals seen in the Autumn. (EAD2)
- To the tune of London bridge is falling down sing 'Autumn leaves are falling down'. Further verses could include 'As we walk we rustle leaves', 'With a rake we gather them'. Encourage children to mime to the words or to provide percussion sound effects. (EAD1)
- Make a role-play tree house (see activity opposite). (EAD2)
- Provide glove puppets of animals that live in trees for children to enjoy using their imaginations, to tell stories in the 'tree house'. (EAD2)

Activity: A role-play tree house

Learning opportunity: Taking part in role play as groups and as individuals.

Early Learning Goal: Expressive Arts and Design. Being imaginative.

Resources: A corner of the room, two low tables or stage blocks, strong string or strong tape, a huge cardboard box (one from a fridge or cooker would be ideal) or a tall roll of corrugated card, green paper, brown and green paint, decorating paint brushes. Old shirts or coveralls for children. 'Home' play equipment such as rugs, tea sets.

Organisation: Involve as many children as possible, a few at a time.

Key vocabulary: Build, paint, tree trunk, leaves, branches, tree house.

What to do: This tree house uses low tables or stage blocks as a platform which allows children to pretend that they are high in a tree house.

Fix the two low tables very securely together using strong string or heavy duty tape such as duct or gaffer tape. Push the tables into a corner to make a raised square platform. Open out the cardboard box and use it to wrap around the tables forming a surround. Mark the places where the table legs are behind the card surround. Make small holes either side of the table legs and thread string through to tie the card in place. Repeat two or three times for each table leg to hold the card very securely. Cut a large entrance hole at table top height.

Now provide children with a large pot of brown paint, some decorators' brushes and some coveralls! Show them how to paint the outside of the card to look like a tree trunk. When the trunk is dry, encourage children to cut out lots of green paper leaf shapes and stick them around the top of the trunk.

Now invite the children to equip the inside of the tree house with home play equipment and to decorate the insides of the walls.

If necessary provide a safe step to help children to clamber in and out of their leafy house.

Activity: Leaf prints

Learning opportunity: Using materials with increasing confidence, control and dexterity.

Early Learning Goal: Physical Development. Moving and handling.

Resources: A selection of leaves, sponges, paint trays or paper plates, ready mix paint in autumn colours, newspaper, paper to print on.

Organisation: Small groups.

Key vocabulary: Sponge, paint, press, print.

What to do: Supply a paper plate or paint tray with a generous amount of paint and a sponge for each colour. Explain that using a separate sponge for each colour will prevent the colours from becoming mixed. Show how to dip the sponge in the paint and to wipe off the excess paint on the side of the plate or tray.

Show the children how to wipe the underside of a leaf with a painted sponge. The leaf is then placed onto the printing paper, painted side down.

Cover the leaf with a piece of newspaper and demonstrate how to gently press the leaf all over to ensure an even print.

Remove the newspaper and the leaf to see the results.

Display

Make a display of cut-out leaf prints mounted on coloured paper. Intersperse them with leaves of the types used for printing. Can children guess which type of leaf made each print?

Theme 4: Autumn Fruits

Communication and Language

- As a group search for books that have pictures of Autumn fruits. Enjoy sharing the stories. (CL1)
- Talk about Autumn fruits that children have seen growing. Where were the fruits? (CL3)
- Describe different Autumn fruits and ask children to identify them from a display. (CL2)
- Place a fruit in a 'feely bag'. Encourage children to describe what they can feel and to identify the fruit. (CL3)

Physical Development

- Using balls and bean bags to represent Autumn fruits play games in which children are squirrels collecting nuts to store away. How many 'nuts' can children gather with one hand. Can they throw and catch the nuts? Can they throw the nuts into a bucket? (PD1)
- Use climbing apparatus to be squirrels climbing trees. (PD1)
- Use snack time to share pieces of fruit, which have been prepared by an adult. (NB Check for food allergies) Talk about the importance of eating fruit as part of a healthy diet and also, the need to wash hands before eating. (PD2)

Personal, Social and Emotional Development

- Talk about fruits and berries and the danger of picking things we do not know are safe. (PSE2)
- Invite children to talk about their favourite fruits. Which fruit flavour drinks or ice creams do they prefer? Encourage children to listen carefully to the ideas of others, understanding that they may be different from their own. (PSE1, 3)

Literacy

- Write Autumn fruit acrostics where each letter in the fruit starts with a new word or phrase e.g.

    Angry
    Cats
    Only
    Read
    New books (L2)

- Explore simple recipes books. Write recipes for squirrels that have Autumn fruits within the ingredients. (L2)

Mathematics

- Use conkers as non-standard units for measuring weight (see activity opposite). (M1, 2)
- Use this addition finger rhyme. (M1)

Rustling through leaves on an Autumn day,
(*Children mime walking through leaves*)
I found a conker in my way.
I picked it up and polished with delight
(*Pretend to pick it up and polish*)
My one brown conker(s) shined so bright.
(*Hold up one finger*)
Continue to two, three, four conkers and so on.

Understanding the World

- Use the internet to research pictures of Autumn fruits. Discover which animals like to eat specific fruits. (UW3)
- Collect sycamore seeds. Encourage children to drop them and to observe and describe how they fall. Make paper gyros and observe how they spin like sycamore seeds (see activity opposite). (UW2)
- Taste exotic fruits. (UW2)
- Plant bulbs in preparation for Spring. (UW2)

Expressive Arts and Design

- Use sunflower seeds, pips and so on to make pictures. Encourage children to look closely at the seeds and discuss what the seeds would grow into if they were planted. (EAD1)
- Cut a selection of fruits in half and use them as printing blocks. Talk about the patterns which the fruit sections make. (EAD1)

● Use tissue paper and textiles to make a collage of favourite fruits. Encourage children to talk about why they are their favourites and to match colours accurately. (EAD1)

Activity: Sycamore seeds and paper gyros

Learning opportunity: Investigating the way sycamore seeds and paper gyros spin as they fall.

Early Learning Goal: Understanding the World. The world.

Resources: Sycamore seeds, paper with gyros pre-drawn (see diagram).

Organisation: Groups of up to 4 children.

Key vocabulary: Sycamore seed, spinning, falling, wings.

What to do: Show children a sycamore seed. Discuss that it is a seed which comes from a sycamore tree. Drop the seed and ask children to describe the way it falls. Encourage them to notice the way it spins.

Show children how to cut out a paper gyro, bend the 'wings' and attach a paper clip to the end. Drop the gyro. Ask them what they notice.

Encourage children to investigate the paper gyros. What happens if they bend the wings the other way? What happens if they add more clips? Discuss how the gyros are similar to the sycamore seeds.

(NB Children should not stand on chairs to drop their gyros.)

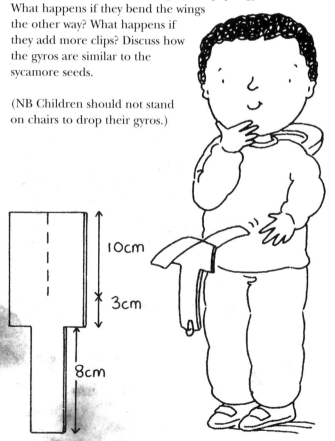

Activity: Conkers as non-standard units

Learning opportunity: Using conkers as a means of measuring weight.

Early Learning Goal: Mathematics. Numbers. Shape, space and measures.

Resources: Collection of conkers, pan or bucket balances, soft toys.

Organisation: Children working in small groups.

Key vocabulary: Same as, more than, less than, balance, heavy, weight.

What to do: Invite children to handle a medium-sized soft toy. Talk about how they would describe the feel of the toy. Children will talk about its texture or the material it is made from. Encourage the conversation to a discussion of the weight of the toy. Would the children say it was heavy or light? How heavy? Explain that one way of describing how heavy something is, is to compare its weight to something else. The toy is as heavy as ....

Now introduce the conkers. Encourage the children to feel how heavy they are. Are they lighter or heavier than the toy? How many conkers do the children think would weigh the same as the toy?

Place the toy in one pan or bucket of a beam balance. Make sure the children understand the principal of how it works. How do we know when the objects in the two pans or buckets are the same weight? Relate the idea to children's experiences of playing on a see saw.

Invite children to balance the toy by placing conkers in the other pan or bucket. Encourage them to add conkers one or two at a time, watching for the buckets to balance. How will they know when they have added too many? How near were their guesses? What else could the children 'weigh' with conkers?

Display

Use the balancing with conkers activity to form the basis of an interactive display. Place the pan or bucket balances on a low table and provide conkers and a collection of objects to weigh. Put the 'squirrel recipes' in clear plastic wallets to make a recipe book. Encourage the children to use the recipes in a role-play home or for 'cooking' in the sand tray.

Theme 5: Wind

Communication and Language

- Read a poem about the wind such as 'Wind' from *Out and About* by Shirley Hughes. Encourage the children to talk about how it feels to be out for a walk in the wind. What sorts of things does the wind blow about? (CL3)
- Use plastic, 'squeezy' bottles as wind, to blow paper around obstacles such as skittles or bean bags. Encourage the children to follow instructions for where to blow the paper. (CL2)

Physical Development

- Play a kite follow-my-leader game in which the children are a kite's tail. Use a large space in which the 'kite' can move in a variety of directions and at changing speeds. Explain that the tail is attached to the kite and that they must move exactly as the kite does. (PD1)
- Enjoy blow painting (see activity opposite). (PD1)

Personal, Social and Emotional Development

- Tell the traditional story of the wind and sun arguing over who is strongest. Discuss the need to be sensitive to others feelings. Use the story as stimulus for role-play (see activity opposite). (PSE2)
- Use jigsaws made from kite-shaped coloured card to encourage children to work together and to take turns. (PSE1, 3)

Literacy

- Read a story about the wind such as *The Wind Blew* by Pat Hutchins. Give children clouds cut from paper on whihc to write words to describe the wind on a windy Autumn day. (L2)
- Talk about activities that are fun to do on a windy day such as flying a kite. Write down the children's ideas. On subsequent days encourage children to read the sentences and to write new ones. (L1, 2)

Mathematics

- Make flags from straws and paper with numbers up to 10 on them. Encourage children to put them in number order. (M1)
- Provide a range of paper shapes from which children can make a triangular flag, a square flag and so on. (M2)
- Decorate kite-shaped pieces of paper. Encourage children to make tails for their kites in which the papers are arranged in a pattern eg red, yellow, red, yellow. (M2)

Understanding the World

- Go outside on a breezy day with paper streamers. Encourage children to investigate how the wind blows the streamers. Hang up some of the streamers so they can be observed from inside. (UW2)
- Attach sails made from straws, tape and paper to small plastic tubs. Float these in long seed trays or the water tray. Encourage children to investigate how the boats can be moved by blowing them. (UW2)

Expressive Arts and Design

- Make shakers filled with a variety of seeds. Compare the different sounds they make. Investigate how one shaker can be played quietly and loudly. Use the shakers to simulate a soft breeze turning into a storm and then back to a breeze. Attach streamers to the shakers and use them for a wind dance. (EAD2)
- Use finger painting to make swirling, windy patterns. (EAD2)

Activity: Wind and sun

Learning opportunity: Listening to a story and using it as focus for discussion and role play.

Early Learning Goal: Personal, Social and Emotional Development. Managing feelings and behaviour.

Resources: A cloak.

Organisation: Whole group sitting on the floor around the story teller.

Key vocabulary: Wind, blew, harder, sun, strongest, warm, hot, hotter.

What to do: Tell children the story of the sun discussing with the wind who is the strongest.

They have a competition to see who can make a man take off the cloak he is wearing. First the wind blows harder and harder. The man just holds on tightly to his cloak.

Then the sun shines down on the man. He becomes so hot that he takes off his cloak. The sun wins!

Talk about what the wind feels like when it blows. How can we tell how hard the wind is blowing? What do we feel like in the sun? Who do children think won the competition? What does it feel like when we argue? What does it feel like to win or lose?

Ask three children to take on the roles of the sun, the wind and the man and enact the story. Encourage children to think about the feelings of the characters.

Activity: Blow painting

Learning opportunity: Using increasing control in using a 'blow' action to direct the flow of paint.

Early Learning Goal: Physical Development. Moving and handling.

Resources: At least one drinking straw per child, runny paint (strong colours) in open tubs, a teaspoon for each colour of paint, paper.

Organisation: children working as individuals in a small group.

Key vocabulary: Blow, push, runny, liquid, blow hard, blow gently.

What to do: Show the children how to use a teaspoon to place a puddle of paint (about the size of a ten pence piece) in the middle of their sheet of paper. They are then going to make the paint spread over the paper by blowing it through the drinking straw.

To do this effectively they will need to blow 'along' the paint rather than down on to it, so the straw needs to be held at a low angle, almost parallel to the paper. Ensure that the children understand the need to blow rather than suck!

As the children blow encourage them to talk about the patterns they are making. How can they make the paint travel more quickly or more slowly? How tiny can they make their 'branches' of paint?

Display

Cover a notice board with sky coloured paper. With the children's help, display the kites and the clouds of wind words. On a table in front, place the sentences describing activities for windy days and the shakers. Display the finger paintings on a separate board as a giant patchwork.

Them 6: Autumn Gallery

(NB In some areas activities have been included which relate to Bonfire Night. Clearly these should only be used where children have previous knowledge of fireworks. This might be through attending a safe, organised firework display or watching fireworks on television.)

Communication and Language

- Talk about the Autumn Gallery. Together make a list of all the jobs that will need to be done such as writing labels and making food. Practise showing visitors around the gallery. (CL3)
- Tell a story about a firework celebration such as 'Paddington and the Bonfire' in *More About Paddington* by Michael Bond. Encourage the children to anticipate what will happen. (CL1)

Physical Development

- Use a tambourine to simulate the sound of a firework being lit, slowly burning until it is a mass of sizzling sparks ending with a loud bang. Encourage children to move in time to the tambourine. They could begin as a small curled up ball, then be lit fireworks in which arms and legs move in rhythmic circles. On the bang children should jump as high as they can, land gently and curl once more into a ball. (PD1)
- Talk about Catherine wheels. Encourage children to use hoops to be Catherine wheels. They could try spinning the hoop around their waists or arms or simply use it for bowling and catching. (PD1)

Personal, Social and Emotional Development

- Several of the activities in this section refer to fireworks. At all times the dangers of playing with fireworks should be emphasised. Many children will, however, have experience of safe enjoyment of fireworks in family or organised events. (PSE2)
- Discuss the way visitors to the Autumn Gallery will need to behave. Can they touch the exhibits? Talk about 'looking with eyes, not hands'. Make a group set of rules for how to behave in the Autumn Gallery. (PSE2)

Literacy

- Talk about art galleries. In galleries there are guides who help visitors to find their way around and who answer questions. They wear name labels. Provide each child with a label to write their name on and decorate. (L2)
- Make posters for the Autumn Gallery. (L2)

- Ask children to suggest words to describe the way fireworks look and sound. Ask them to write the words on paper cut in the shapes of fireworks.(L1)

Mathematics

- Encourage children to help with the mounting and putting up of the Autumn displays. Discuss the shapes of pictures and the size of mounts needed for them. (M2)
- Use the displays as a focus for the development of positional language: Next to, above, between, below etc. Ask questions such as 'Whose picture is next to Lloyd's?'. (M2)

Understanding the World

- Cover apples with melted chocolate and decorate with popcorn, vermicelli etc. Encourage children to observe how the chocolate melts and sets. Why does it melt? (UW2)
- Use a variety of 'found' natural materials, such as fir cones, acorns, hazelnut cases or twigs, to make models. Incorporate some commercial materials such as cleaned feathers, sequins or pipe cleaners to add extra features. As the children work talk about the materials they are using. Where did they come from? (UW2)
- Make traditional bonfire food – gingerbread (see activity opposite). (UW2)

Expressive Arts and Design

- Make rockets from cardboard tubes to hang from the ceiling. (EAD2)
- On black paper make splatter pictures of exploding fireworks. (EAD1)
- Talk about colours which show up well at night. Cover card stars on both sides with glitter, shiny paper, sequins, etc and hang them up. (EAD1)
- Collaborate to make firework collages for the Autumn Gallery (see activity opposite). (EAD2)

Activity: Making gingerbread

Learning opportunity: Experiencing mixing and handling materials with opportunities to make and discuss observations.

Early Learning Goal: Understanding the World. The world.

Resources: Ingredients for recipe below, rolling pins, cutters, dried fruit to decorate.

Organisation: Children in groups of up to four with adult support.

Key vocabulary: Mix, pour, stir, roll, words to describe the appearance, texture and smells of the dough, before, during and after baking.

What to do: For approximately 30 children:
750g (24 oz) plain flour
10ml (2 teaspoons) bicarbonate of soda
20 ml (4 teaspoons) ground ginger
250g (8oz) chopped butter
375g (12 oz) soft light brown sugar
120ml (8 tablespoons) golden syrup
2 eggs, beaten
Dried fruit to decorate

Make sure that everyone has washed their hands.

Mix the sifted flour, bicarbonate of soda and ginger in a large bowl. Rub in the butter until the mixture is like breadcrumbs. In a separate bowl beat the syrup into the eggs. Stir this into the flour mixture. Mix to a firm dough.

When helping to make the dough encourage the children to talk about the feel, appearance and smell of each ingredient as it is added. How does the mixture change after each addition?

This dough can be squashed, pummelled, pinched and kneaded almost indefinitely. It is extremely good tempered!

Show the children how to roll the dough and to use the cutters to make shapes. Allow them to use their own ideas in using the fried fruit to decorate.

Place each child's finished gingerbread on a separate, named piece of baking parchment on a baking tray.

Bake in a pre-heated oven, 180°C, Mark 4, for ten minutes.

Cool on a rack, then enjoy tasting!

Activity: Firework collage

Learning opportunity: Collaborating to make collages.

Early Learning Goal: Expressive Arts and Design. Being imaginative.

Resources: Pictures of fireworks exploding in the sky, pieces of black paper, chalks, pastels or bright paints, shiny collage materials, glue.

Organisation: Whole group discussion followed by children working as individuals.

Key vocabulary: Firework, explode, bright, sparkle, shine, words to describe the sounds and appearance of fireworks.

What to do: Ask who has seen fireworks. What kinds of fireworks were they? Did they make sounds? What did they look like when they were lit? Which fireworks were children's favourites?

Look at the collected firework pictures. What fireworks can they see? Talk about the kinds of fireworks which children may have seen and heard such as sparklers, rockets, Catherine wheels and Roman candles. Ask them to suggest words to describe how the fireworks looked, behaved and sounded?

Talk about the ways in which some fireworks are named: Golden Rain, Silver Fountain, Volcano, Space Rocket. Why do the children think these names were chosen?

Explain that they are going to make a large firework picture for the Autumn Gallery. Encourage each child to make a firework collage on their piece of black paper, using a range of sparkly materials, pastels, chalk and paint.

Display

Display all the firework collages together to make one large frieze, along with the words which children wrote to describe the appearance, sounds and names of the fireworks. Encourage children to read the words. Invite suggestions for additional, descriptive words to add to the display.

Bringing it all together

The Autumn Gallery

Explain to the children that in a few days time you are going to hold an Autumn Gallery. Talk to the children about galleries and exhibitions, explaining what the words mean. Have any of the children ever been to a museum, or seen a gallery of children's work on a television art programme? The children are going to make a gallery of their work for visitors to enjoy.

The gallery can be prepared as part of a morning or afternoon session, with guests joining the children later to admire the exhibits and share some refreshments.

You will need to plan the sessions to allow time for producing work for display and other preparations. Explain to children right at the beginning of the Autumn themed activities that they are working towards a gallery, so that some work will be put away to be kept safely. If your usual practice is that all work is taken home at the end of each session, you will need to ask children whether you may keep their work until after the exhibition. Make sure that the children understand that all their work will be taken home eventually. Continue to allow some work to go home, saving just one or two 'special' pieces of work for each child. If necessary arrange with parents/carers for individual pieces to be returned to you for display. It is important that children retain 'ownership' of their work.

Think about the work you have to show and how best to display it. It may fall into fairly clear categories or themes. If wall space is limited, flatwork can be displayed on garden trellis or large sheets of covered card. Models will need a table or large covered box. Think about combining 2-D and 3-D work, and use boxes of different shapes to make plinths, which children can help to cover and decorate. Keep a checklist of items on display, making sure that every child has at least one contribution in the gallery.

Making preparations

The introductory discussion will have helped children to understand that there are plenty of jobs to be done.

Food

Depending on the time of day at which the event is taking place, you may decide to provide simple refreshments. Encourage the children to think about what sorts of food and drink might be appropriate. Use the gingerbread recipe to make biscuits for guests. To make a change from the original activity encourage the children to make the biscuits in different shapes such as Autumn leaves or fruits. Ask the children how they think the biscuits should be stored and served. Decorate paper plates or paper tray covers in Autumn colours and patterns.

Invitations

Encourage the children to think about the sort of information which an invitation needs to give. Talk about the importance of visitors knowing when to come, and for how long the gallery will be open.

How could the invitations be designed to show the Autumn theme?

Encourage children to be adventurous in their ideas.

As children produce cards it is useful to have photocopied information (using children's suggestions) to paste inside them.

Accessories

Involve the children in making labels for their work, including headings for different sections of the displays. Ask the children to help you to word the labels which will give some information about their work. What were these pictures about? What sort of paint did you use?

Remind the children that this information could be important. As guides in the gallery they may need to answer questions. Some information signs may be needed in the gallery. Will visitors know where to collect refreshments or how to find the toilets?

Make a Gallery Open/ Closed sign to go on the door.

Resources

Resources to collect
- A few magazines with recipes or pictures of fruits and vegetables, or gardening catalogues.
- Conkers, sycamore seeds, cones, acorns.
- Examples of fruits, vegetables and breads.
- Baking materials and ingredients (see recipes).

Everyday resources
- Boxes, large and small for modelling.
- Papers and cards of different weights, colours and textures available eg sugar, corrugated card, silver and shiny papers.
- Dry powder paints for mixing and mixed paints for covering large areas such as card tree trunks.
- Different sized paint brushes from household brushes to thin brushes for delicate work and a variety of paint mixing containers.
- A variety of drawing and colouring pencils, crayons, pastels, charcoals.
- Additional decorative and finishing materials such as sequins, foils, glitter, tinsel, shiny wool and threads, beads, pieces of textiles, parcel ribbon.
- Table covers.

Stories
- *Autumn Story* by Jill Barklem
- *After the Storm* by Nick Butterworth
- *More About Paddington* by Michael Bond
- *Titch* by Pat Hitchins
- *Elmer and the Wind* by David McKee
- *The Tale of Squirrel Nutkin* by Beatrix Potter
- *The Gingerbread Man* traditional story
- *The Prickly Hedgehog,* by Mark Ezra and Gavin Rowe

Poems
- *This Little Puffin* by Elizabeth Matterson
- *Out and About* by Shirley Hughes

Resources for planning
- *Planning for Learning through Weather* by Rachel Sparks Linfield
- **England:** Statutory framework for the Early Years Foundation Stage (2012)(www.foundationyears.org.uk/early-years-foundation-stage-2012)
- **Northern Ireland:** CCEA (2011) 'Curricular Guidance for Pre-school Education' (www.rewardinglearning.org.uk/curriculum/pre_school/index.asp) CCEA (2006) Understanding the Foundation Stage(www.nicurriculum.org.uk/docs/foundation_stage/UF_web.pdf)
- **Scotland:** Learning and Teaching Scotland (2010) 'Pre-birth to Three: Positive Outcomes for Scotland's Children and Families' (www.ltscotland.org.uk/earlyyears/). The Scottish Government (2008) 'Curriculum for Excellence: Building the Curriculum 3 – A Framework for Learning and Teaching' (www.ltscotland.org.uk/buildingyourcurriculum/policycontext/btc/btc3.asp)
- **Wales:** Welsh Assembly (2008) 'Framework for Children's Learning for 3 to 7-year-olds in Wales' (http://wales.gov.uk/topics/educationand skills/schoolshome/curriculuminwales/arevised curriculumforwales/foundationphase/?lang=en)

Collecting evidence of children's learning

Monitoring children's development is an important task. Making a profile of children's achievements, strengths, capabilities interests and learning will help you to see progress and will draw attention to those who are having difficulties for some reason. If a child needs additional professional help, such as speech therapy, these cumulative profiles will provide valuable evidence.

Profiles should cover all the areas of learning, as defined by the relevant UK framework, and be the result of collaboration between practitioners, parents and carers. Parents should be made aware of your record keeping policies when their child joins your group. Show parents the types of documentation that you are keeping and make sure they understand their purpose. As a general rule, documentation should be open. Families should have access to their child's documentation at any time and know they can contribute to it. Take regular opportunities to talk to parents about children's progress. If you have formal discussions regarding children about whom you have particular concerns, a dated record of the main points should be kept.

Keeping it manageable

Documentation should be helpful in informing practitioners, adult helpers and parents and always be for the benefit of the child. The golden rule is to keep it simple, manageable and useful. Do not try to make records following every activity!

Documentation will basically fall into two categories – observations and reflections:

Observations

- **Spontaneous observations:** Sometimes you will want to make a note of observations as they happen e.g. a child is heard counting cars accurately during a play activity, or is seen to play collaboratively for the first time.

- **Planned observations:** Sometimes you will plan to make observations of children's developing skills within a planned activity. Using the learning opportunity identified for an activity will help you to make appropriate judgments about children's capabilities, strengths and interests, and to record them systematically.

To collect information:

- Talk to children about their activities and listen to their responses.
- Listen to children talking to each other.
- Observe children's work such as early writing, drawings, paintings and models. (Keeping photocopies or photographs can be useful in tracking progress. Photographs are particularly useful to monitor children's development in the outdoor environment.)

Sometimes it may be appropriate to set up 'one off' activities for the purposes of monitoring development. Some groups at the beginning of each term, for example, ask children to write their name and to make a drawing of themselves to record their progressing skills in both co-ordination and observation.

Reflections

It is useful to spend regular time reflecting on the children's progress. Aim to make some comments about each child each week, and discuss these regularly with colleagues and families.

Informing your planning

Collecting evidence about children's progress is time consuming and it is important that it is useful. When planning, use the information collected to help you to decide what learning opportunities you need to provide next for each child. For example, a child who has poor pencil or brush control will benefit from more play with dough or construction toys to build strength of muscles in the hands and fingers.

Example observation sheet

Name: Lucy Field

Date: 17.1.13

Area of Learning: Mathematics. Count reliably with numbers from 1 to 20.

Context (Please tick):

Child-initiated: √   **Adult-led:**

Alone: **In a group:** √

Observation: Lucy is playing outside with two friends. She is trying to build the tallest tower and counting the bricks. "1, 2, 3, 4, 5, 7, 8. Mine's 8. Yours is only 7." She knocks the tower down, chuckles and starts to build again, counting as she places the bricks. "1, 2, 3, 4, 5, 7." The tower falls over. "Oh blow. I wanted to do 20."

What next: Check Lucy knows 6 follows 5. Encourage use of the outdoor counting grids, skittles and number rhyme CD.

Observer: E. M. Hogg

Overview of areas covered through 'Autumn'

	Communication and Language	Physical Development	Personal, Social and Emotional Development	Literacy	Mathematics	Understanding the World	Expressive Arts and Design
Detecting Autumn	Listening and attention Understanding Speaking	Moving and handling Health and self-care	Self-confidence and self-awareness Managing feelings and behaviour Making relationships	Reading Writing	Numbers Shape, space and measures	People and communities The world Technology	Exploring and using media and materials Being imaginative
Harvest	Listening and attention Understanding Speaking	Moving and handling Health and self-care	Self-confidence and self-awareness Managing feelings and behaviour Making relationships	Reading Writing	Numbers Shape, space and measures	People and communities The world Technology	Exploring and using media and materials Being imaginative
Autumn Leaves	Listening and attention Understanding Speaking	Moving and handling Health and self-care	Self-confidence and self-awareness Managing feelings and behaviour Making relationships	Reading Writing	Numbers Shape, space and measures	People and communities The world Technology	Exploring and using media and materials Being imaginative
Autumn Fruits	Listening and attention Understanding Speaking	Moving and handling Health and self-care	Self-confidence and self-awareness Managing feelings and behaviour Making relationships	Reading Writing	Numbers Shape, space and measures	People and communities The world Technology	Exploring and using media and materials Being imaginative
Wind	Listening and attention Understanding Speaking	Moving and handling Health and self-care	Self-confidence and self-awareness Managing feelings and behaviour Making relationships	Reading Writing	Numbers Shape, space and measures	People and communities The world Technology	Exploring and using media and materials Being imaginative
Autumn Gallery	Listening and attention Understanding Speaking	Moving and handling Health and self-care	Self-confidence and self-awareness Managing feelings and behaviour Making relationships	Reading Writing	Numbers Shape, space and measures	People and communities The world Technology	Exploring and using media and materials Being imaginative

Note: For each theme, highlight the Early Learning Goal areas covered through both adult focused and child-initiated activities relating to 'Autumn'.

Home links

The theme of Autumn lends itself to useful links with children's families. Through working together children and adults gain respect for each other and build comfortable and confident relationships.

Establishing partnerships

- Keep parents informed about the theme for Autumn, and the activities for each week. By understanding the work of the group, parents will enjoy the involvement of contributing ideas, time and resources.
- Request parental permission before taking children out of the group on an Autumn walk. Describe your route and the purposes of the activity. Additional parental help will be necessary for this activity to be carried out safely.
- Photocopy the Family page for each child to take home.
- Invite friends, childminders and families to share the 'Autumn Gallery'.

Visiting enthusiasts

- Invite a parent, carer or friend who is a keen gardener to come into the group to talk about Autumn jobs in the garden. Perhaps they could bring examples of vegetables or fruits they have grown to show to the children.
- Invite adults from other cultures to show children how some of the less familiar fruits and vegetables are used in traditional recipes.

Resource requests

- Encourage contributions of Autumn 'finds' from family walks.
- Ask to borrow Autumn coloured fabrics or seasonal pictures which could be used for displays.

Preparing the Autumn Gallery

- Invite enthusiastic cooks to help during the activities involving gingerbread or chocolate apple making.